The Alphabet Poetry Book

by

Kenneth Yocus

To: Cal;
Health! Wealth!
Happiness!
Sincerely; Kenneth Yocus

RoseDog❧Books
PITTSBURGH, PENNSYLVANIA 15222

ISBN: 978-1-4349-8188-2
eISBN: 978-1-4349-4432-0
Printed in the United States of America

First Printing

For more information or to order additional books, contact:
RoseDog Books
701 Smithfield Street
Pittsburgh, Pennsylvania 15222
U.S.A.
1-800-834-1803
www.rosedogbookstore.com

Dedication
June 20, 2002

I wish to extend my most thoughtful condolence to my friends, family, and the love of my life. They have been most thoughtful with the selection, quality, and choice of the words. Thank you, all, for the help that was provided.

Very Truly Yours,

Kenneth Yocus

Alphabet Poetry

Aglet
11-20-2007

Here is a cord
to tie in a knot
loop upon loop
can you afford
to pick up a dime on a dot?

Have you ever
worn a braid on your shoulder,
or rolled down a boulder
from a hill?

Moss grows on a rock
a mountain has a peak.
Put on your socks and
don't tie your laces in a knot.

Tag the cord, color the braid.

The mountain has a peak.
There are rubber soles on the sneakers.

So that you can leave a streak.
When do you run up the hill,
and kick up dust on the road?

A tagged cord
on the shoulder of your ornament
secured with the end of a lace
reminds me of a place
I used to go.

When I wanted to know
about the shoes
in the showcase.

Green string
and all sorts of white and purple
and brown trinkets
dangle from the chain
of the necklace.

It is a very personal thing.

Aqueduct
01-03-05

Water from a distance
without persistence
flows fluently
and is consistent.

The source
of course
is because of the force
of the funnel through the tunnel.

Across the canal
I can see very well to be
where the water
flows through the trees
foretells the breach of the boat and the bow.

Passage through the structure
I wonder with closure
when there will be an obstruction
because of the lightning, the rain,
and the thunder.

Clearly, can you see the pipe
about to burst?
The swell of the seam is ripe
it will be costly to repair
There will be an abundance
of thirst!

A Quiet Day
06-15-2000

Every moment without you
is like
an eternity in time

a second
seems like a minute

a minute
seems like an hour

an entire day
appears to me
as if a lunar month
has flown by

a month lasts
forever
in my mind

My thoughts
are infinitely
about you

I cannot wait
until I can
see you tomorrow.

Asshole
03-03-2003

What is the common wild ass?
Is it domesticated?
or kind of stupid, silly, or crass
past resemblance of having
longer ears
or a shorter mane
completely insane?

Deep in the pit
Hallowed out
a squalid place
whence there is zit
I wanted to spit
at it.

When the ball is to be hit
into distinct sections
of a course
deal with it face down
with bit and force.

Which one particle
nucleon or electron
at adjacent states
above and below
are frequently occupied
there is a recurrent receptacle
put into place beside
the article.

At a spot, on or near the hole
On the drive from the tee
shut oneself in or behind
up or near a sizable tree
a depression into the surface untold.

The open space in a thing
derived and equivalent to a cavity
also to be applied
in or through digging.

A flaw a fault
could halt, the excavation
of the wall of expectation.

The general word
for an open space
is the place
for an extension
within a solid body absurd
in taste.

Within a solid body
Whether or not it extends
a sizable amount
of prick holes
the short stop
is the sodomy.

Belmont
03-26-2000

We care for each other always.
You activate my start button and I push yours.

Together we line up linearly.

Leg to leg
Arm to arm
Breast to breast
Cheek to cheek
Tongue to tongue.

Our anticipation is immense
the sweat is salty and sweet
as if we were tasting flesh
raw and red and purple and pink
and orange and bright and blue
from our heat.

Toes tickle toes
fingers mingle with fingers
nails begin to scratch.
There is a streak of stream
an almost inaudible wine.

The rush is on
to finish the starting line
to what we have begun.

Hair to hair
nose to nose
skin to skin
lip to lip.

The particles are flying everywhere
Our elements combine
We have won the event.

The prize, the purse of no expense.

Bottle
04-06-2006

A bottle of wine
with a glass is fine.
I can taste the flavor
so pure and divine.
For our splendor
we always kind, of remind each other
of a very special valentine.

Holding liquids
as fluid as they can be,
they are distilled spirits
some of them are antiquity.

The capacity of contents
being well spent.
Intent, I went to the distillery.
Can you see clearly, where we are
or must we pretend?

Substitution of mixtures
we must control
and restrain our protocol to consume
and look at the importance of pictures.

I am breathless.
I curtail my need
for the bottle.
So that I may not,
be influenced
by the caresses.

In the colors of my mind
I am painting,
with fluent strokes.
The movement of the bubbles
and the barkeep is ever so kind.

Watching the orchids grow
do you know, how the hops
and barley flow? Perhaps,
you may believe in the
forget-me-nots?

Burden
11-03-2004

One has to bear, a heavy load
full of duty and responsibility, truly
I am told, not to fear what you hear.

The capacity of the ship
or the weight of its cargo
will oppress the sorrow
and keep a stiff upper lip.

The beast of the burden
all of a sudden
asserted and in dispute.

The accompaniment of a flute
with a trim rudder
breaks the waves
of an urgent closing, uncertain.

Repeat the idea
the theme of the drone
sing a song with the bagpipe
in tune.

Without despair
far or near from the fear
of the misfortune.

Listen to the bumblebee
can you see
in between the flutter of the wings
what is to swing
in the forest, in the trees?

It is a heavy burden:
I am closing the curtain
do not swear
I hear
the call of the wild
So close and so far.

That age are those for who are
watching the trouble?

Beyond the rubble and rock
is the forgotten omen.

Coral
12-07-2000

How composed I am
of your glowing substance
I am a hard skeleton
without you.

My presence is plenty
full of tropical paradise
when I am with you.

I am soaked
with mere outlines
of my framework without you.

You provide my support
of reddish yellow, green, white,
and blue essence of existence.

Planted within the bottom
of the sea
is a spectrum
of coral for you and me.

The meaning of our movement
is flooded with feeling
our foundation is forever
inside each other.

Curly
06-21-2006

To adorn with
or as if, we were
to lie down cozily
curled up in a passionate
state of bliss.

Can we play the game
move and progress,
as if we were to caress
our life together
as if things were the same?

A weight is raised
from the level of the thighs,
are you surprised?
From the look in your eyes
I feel as if you are pleased.

As in an expression
a corner of the lip,
taught with the raising of the hips
is it compassion for each other
or procrastination?

The ringlets in your hair
as if to appear brushed up
so fair with their flow
are nowhere near to compare
in a cup.

Lay down frantically
and bundle up with a good book.
As you flutter through the pages
think of how easy,
you may appear to be, in
your sentimentality.

The pink rose
is always so close
to me.

only because of your
eternal hospitality.

Death
10-24-2004

From the beginning
to the end
can you see
where I have gone
what I was to be?

Am I in a black robe, forbid
upright and rigid with my scythe
holding my skeleton?

The culmination
and anticipation of the injection
is bitter cold I am told with a probe.

The murder of the pestilence
and the chemicals of the substance:
I feel the resilience: Everywhere!

Am I immune to my living existence?

That was the cause?
Could it have been prevented?
Was it murder with extreme procrastination?

I pause, with serious contemplation,
if temptation is damnation.

Debt
10-20-2003

As a matter of habit
I want to return
what is prevalent
to it.

There is an obligation
to pay or return
what I have earned
unfortunately to the situation.

Giving rise to an increase
or a decrease
in the liability
considerably.

Truly an entry
to be entirely satisfactory
for whatever the barter
may be.

The condition of owing
the net worth
of showing
we shall see
our paying
with our productivity
of course cautiously
continually.

Dirt
03-12-2008

Where loose soil of the earth
upon the planet,
from hence we are inhabitants,
the honeysuckle flowers grow.

There are green foliage blooming
everywhere,
in the dust,
mud, and grime,
mixed with spoiling dirt.

A relatively large amount,
of a malicious nature
obscene and lewd.

From one who lends unscrupulous
fortune to those extremely impoverished
is undesirable and unpleasant
Those are the circumstances
that of which we are all about.

Spreading or imparting dirt,
dust to dust,
exhibits all of the mixtures
for us to exploit, extremely absurd.

In clouds of smoke
thinking of a joke,
that is funny to tell,
it is kind of swell.

When the water is in the well
and the spoke
of the wheels,
kicks up the dirt
and the dust

is in the air,
and you see the smoke,
a thunderbolt of lightning may
kiss and tell,
about how swell
soil is for always
letting the flowers flow.

Spinning and spreading
watching the dirt
twist and turn
so that the blue-green grass grows.

Dream
04-24-2006

I had a dream
passing through my mind.
My emotions have gone wild,
or so it may seem,
to be that way.
Can you understand what it may mean?

In a very remote way
imagine as possible,
most desirable and ideal
some word you may say,
to bring joy, as you gaze
upon a star.
Someday on a very special holiday
no matter where you are
can you hear, see, and feel
where you may be, clearly?

How beautiful are the colors
of green?
The flowers.
The trees.
The leaves.
The light beams, through everything.

An aspiration,
is a motivation,
to see a vision
in your imagination.

I want to pass and spend
to the very end
of my ambition,
a fancy feast of fruition,
upon conclusion
of my delusion, of my dream.

Around and around,
I go,
where my dream may wander
I do not know.
I am thinking of ice cream.

Emasculate
01-31-2003

I have the power
To reproduce, with strength and force
The glass, can become course
on the hour
well endowed, and how
can I specify intercourse?

With virility:
in truth and censorship
hip to hip, sweat to sweat, brow to brow
extreme sensitivity.

As by motion of hand to hand
can we understand
the endowment and comprehend
What you and I have spent?
Skin and fluids flowing intense
on the squeeze we are perturbed
and immense to please
each other with climatic eruption
for our need of orgasmic combustion.

Emotions of astronomical explosion
conclusive to the heat of passionate
possession.

Our pulse is quick
and full of pulsation.

Esther
04-30-03

The reaction of the situation
is formed with a radial
of an intrinsic medium
that its compound
end creates a storm.

So precious and few
are the moments
that we have shared, I cared
for her conscientious objection.

Colors of the spectrum
always new mixtures of pictures
I knew how true
I could be to me, carefully
we would see our future intimately
before we departed so preciously.

Always, a pleasure
never a chore, before
we rode the waves, of the shore
together, maternally to endure.

Forever searching
for a place, a space
out of our confinement
we found temporary contentment.

Her smile was bright and cheerful
meaningful, persuasive, and delightful,
always thoughtful
pleasant and peaceful
perpendicular to a peculiar
politeness of persistence.

Excellent
05-24-2004

Keep in mind
it is
one of its kind
with merit
all of the time
it is not necessary
to rewind
and again use a rhyme.

Packing breakable things
it seems
unmistakable
stuffing
and shaving, trimming
new beginnings.

The trademark
is perfection
without exception
you must not talk
about a correction.

Used as a motto
the state of the seal
it is not real
to say I ought to.

It is good
surpassing virtue
lofty and high
I ask myself why
As I should!

Frigid
05-24-2004

I am told
that it is extremely frigid;
therefore, my bones are rigid.

Abnormally repelled
I can tell
I am not well
breathing.

The heat of the warmth
I am bored with words
that are wrinkled
and torn.

Stiff and formal
I can assure you
to be awful
and also contradict myself
allows oneself to be cordial.

Habitually
Consistency
Indefinitely
Frosty and flaky

Grief
09-26-2002

I am suffering intensely
emotionally at a loss
a deep and acute sadness
recourse?

The pain is potentially hard
and subject to sorrow
a morrow
a misfortune of my mind
madness.

My mourning of injury
Is a heavy burden to fail
If I am ruined
can I prevail?

Afflicted with distress
I am under duress
Is this reason enough
I ask?

How many times
Can I endure
the pain, the hardship
the tomorrow, the task?

Hack
12-01-2001

It is a harsh road I ride
Irresistible, irregular people
With sweeping strokes I shape and trim
chop and cut the crude pride.

To carry out successfully
breakup with a hoe
raffle and knock, rock and roll
Uptown—Downtown Eastside—Westside
I'm in a hurry
All around town
If you get me there quick
Then we both need not worry.

I strike my arm
for the opponent
I kick my leg
on the shins
off we go
with dry harsh coughs
I hack and grin.

There is a tool
for a slash, a gash a notch
made by a sharp instrument.
It is called the human element
irregular are the cuts.
For the fool, a simple rule
Steady progressive increments.

As I am drying out
and grating the streets
I am holding my place
for the people I meet.

A brick is solid, as a rock
unburned and set, out to dry.
It is a place on a hack
For a falcon to cry.
In solitude and servitude
I crack and break
it out of the lock, the key
for the fare I take.

Hand
11-05-2003

Grasping and gripping
below the wrist
I insisted with the sense
of my fist
to rip apart
what I started to twist.

Including the palm
the pincer-like claw
hence, basic to seize
what I need to clasp
in a manner in which
I am within my past.

Used in skill
with dexterity and posterity
sincerely the promise
to fulfill matrimony
in influential will
Can I remain still?

Let us applause the appearance
a signature of performance
indicating a cluster
of ignorance.

Transfer directly
the original source
with nothing left over
from the course
of previous force.

I declare my intentions
before my prevention
of nothing left over
to refuse my manner

of objection.
From hand to mouth
I bequeath diligently
constantly, without exception
I bite my teeth and trim my nails
to perfection.

Let's pass along
with agreement and cooperation
our situation to become
without effort
strong.

On all sides
in all directions
without the preliminaries
there is no sensation
to divide
our intentions.

Immediately
my point of view
with reference
I disclose to propose
spontaneity.

To take in hand
and understand
upon despair
where there is demand
for a band of brand
to blend in with.

I hold stern
with arrogance and concern
I turn my head to see
what can not be
severity, delicately
arbitrary, combining form
and in heavy manner firm!

Hat
06-12-2007

I take my hat off to you.
with my brim in hand
I understand, how sweet it is
for you to be true.
How clear that may be is
for a very special clue.

In two or more positions
it is a kind of situation
in more than one capacity,
to question your curiosity,
about your disposition,
in relation to the inquisition,
about how to wear your hat.

How about the crown
so bright in the light?

with your Easter bonnet
a blue true color,
an emerald within a blanket
around the flavor of forever
with the flow of cologne
your hat fits flossy
with forget-me-nots.

Two or more positions
humbly and respectfully
clearly and sincerely,
in all of the situations,
I wear my hat.

Bring on the band
with all of the colorful ribbons.
we all understand
about the fact as to
how to wear our hat!

with a shaped covering
there is always something
to say to a very special person
who has nothing to portray,
when the top of the cap is not showing.

Incurable
06-01-2000

We share each other's dreams
hopes, ambitions
desires, fantasies
and pleasures.

I think of us as
Romeo and Juliet
Samson and Delilah
Caesar and Cleopatra
John Smith and Pocahontas.

To me, loving someone
means never having to say your sorry.

I will never be sorry for having met
someone like you.

One evening when we are together,
gazing into distant space,
we may see a shooting star.

I would wish for us to be together
forever in love.

I am incurably romantic for you.
My most precious, pristine princess.

Insouciant
11-04-2002

Are you calm and unbothered?
Can you see the quiet
before the storm?
are the waters still and calm
or are we indubitably regarded
as turbulent and further
away from our silent warmth?

Earnestly, carefree
I propose prostitution
to seek and approach
attempt to entice purposely.

Is it immoral
Is it wrong
to hum and sing a song
of solicitation?

For donations
You must be a member
pleadingly forever, impersonations
of character, representations.

Ask for your appeal
of only real, invasions
super natural interpretations
of being here.

Jesus
03-10-2004

In the name of our Lord
Jesus Christ
Let it not be told
To mention the name
in vain.

Beware of the poltergeist
The young and the old, be bold.

Founder of the religion
a masculine name
it is profane
to believe in adventitious
superstition.

Spread over
and be clear of
what you hear
from ear to ear
beware
of the power.

Originally a title
later used as part of the name.
I feel the pain
as the riddle
of the insane
do not belittle
and light the flame!

Regarded as the Christian
whence the appearance
is the cause of the effect!

In sequence
the circumstance
the substance
the endurance
will be the prevalence!

The Messiah
is prophesied
there is no compromise
amen, amen, amen
halleluiah!

In the Old Testament
Jesus of Nazareth
later used
as part of the name
Christ
in contentment.

Kenneth
04-08-2004

Me, myself, and I
apple pie
football, hot dogs, and Chevrolet
what can I say?

Let me look forward
to a cheerful and bright day!

I know and you know
what is below
and above
the perception
and the range of the distribution
entails understanding the condition
blow for blow.

Can you look and see?
eventually
carefully, cautiously
how can I be free?

Who knew what was true
do you?
What is my fortune, and
am I confidently capable
of being in tune?

Leviathan
06-12-2009

The size is the power of a monster.
Huge as an animal
rolling up and down
as if you were taking a ride
on a roller coaster.

You can hit and thrash
wiggle and wobble
beat soundly
but can you make a big splash?

Horizontally
and flattened by the head
like a slice of baked bread.
Fine of its kind
it is totally
vertically huge in reality.

Forelimbs and flippers
they are free
to splash the waves
that are green and blue and white.

Flip and flop
the tall ships swerve
and the sailors
will have kippers.

The Cherokee can see
clearly through the immense and huge
order of the mammal
perfectly.

Snapdragons
grow in the green fields
under the blue sky.

A whale or a shark
would hide in the dark.
Afraid of the huge enormous
ignition of the spark,
of a Leviathan.

Love
11-22-02

Am I fond of you
or do you desire me?
Have my dreams come true
or do you design devotion
indefinitely?

The attachment and expression
of affection are passionate,
whence we are strong
with our realization
of tension forevermore.

The object of such liking
is based in part
of such taking
very deep and very hard.

My affection for devout attraction
is a dream come true
because you are a person
to show love, too.

The motion for love
To be embraced, fondled, kissed
to intensely exist
where persists
flight of the dove
regardless of being missed.

Can we play for nothing
or is there an interest
in something monetary, unreasonable
seasonal between everything
implied, that is best
for the sake of testing
our feelings our zest?

The benevolent design of our constitution.
A plant that loves the shade
can be made from our
delight of a man and woman's devotion
forever made, with serious attraction.

I tenderly feel
a powerful infatuation
the connection of intercourse, so real.

Sensitive and deep to feel
What is happening to me?
You are penetrating
my mind
And I am uncertain
As to how much
I can substantiate your
virtue of appeal in kind.

Messenger
02-02-2002

I am on an errand.
What do I carry?
Where am I going?

Something wrapped up in a band.
Whom shall I see?

When I get there,
I know it is bringing
something somewhere.

A persona enveloped
Wrapped up in a string
ready to seal and package
and deliver disheveled anything.

The light-line
definitively, dispatches
passing heavy burden
bumping and banging.

It is yours and mine
The lifeline
he and she watches
the exciting bludgeons
with weight overwhelming
There is a turndown
a rip a tear everywhere
overcome.

New York City
05-18-2004

A knife
A fork
A bottle
and a cork
that's how we spell
New York.

At the mouth of the Hudson
into the five boroughs
who knows
where we will go?

To a party house?
we can lay on the couch
and kiss
and scratch a tooth.

Brooklyn begins
where Queens ends
the brooks bend
the canal curls into the Bronx

where big are the cold turkeys
and the bologna
and how about the curfew
in Queens?
Where the opposite sex meet the Kings
explicitly
In Manhattan
women meet men
and men meet women.

In conclusion,
women go to Richmond
and arrive upon decisions.

Orange
11-23-2003

The groves of orange are there
they are everywhere
for us to see
the rue of the tree.

Having white fragrant blossoms
often carried by brides
with a sweet juicy pulp, inside
flowing from bosoms.

Through faulty ripples
resembling various evergreen
It may seem, beyond all resemblance
the pit that is in the middle.

Plowing from the river
resembling the sweet
bitter citrus
it is ambiguous
to the bite of the bitter.

Any of several
yellow wood
fragrant if understood
to be foreseen
in between bevelment
reddish yellow and round
with upside and down
sometimes green overall.

Ordeal
09-17-2003

Am I accused
of which was supposed to be
for me, a chore
of more than was expected
to succeed.

My trying experience
of exposure
was close to your
deliverance of innocence.

To be divinely protected
from physical danger
is to be expected
of trying anger
indefinitely
consequentially, invented.

The ancient method
of trial and error
is forever within
our ultimate effort.

Whence there is penance
an appearance of persistence
is always present
pleasantly, pertinent
to our
deliverance.

Propulsion
06-17-2002

A driving force
leaping forward, onward I go
the destination, I do not know.

Can you take me there?
Somewhere, anywhere?

It is an act
of pushing and pressing precise
A tension of propulsion
powerful, plentiful, propelling
twirling the blades
that cut through the facts
of facade and ice.

Spin the wheels
and turn the shaft
grind the gears
and have your tears
and fears

cut through the serious shadows
of curious cares.

Roller Coaster
07-29-02

The wheels go 'round and 'round
upside down and inside out
various cylinders grind and crush
and press something smooth and slush
satin and silk and textile found
fabric used for applying the brush.

Spreading ink on the form
a swelling wave that breaks
a long bandage in a roll
it is impressed! In flight it takes!

Numerous heavy swelling.
Spreading caressed.
Specific to shades.
Rolling and tumbling and hopping
clumsily and similar to the roll
the jay, the canary, the trill, the bop.

Dip and curve sharply
open the coaster
the amusement of tracks!
Trace the open space abruptly
boast and brave the wheels tightly.

Metal and wood
hard and soft
bluish easy movement
rubber and draft
various people could sense
the tropical old world
clumsily and fluent.

Secret Solace
04-22-1997

It is done without others
kept from general knowledge

in a manner that prevents them
from being observed or detected

hidden from sight, concealed

esoteric.

Secretive, mouth closed
beyond ordinary human understanding
classified, below top-secret.

Something

A mystery of nature
not readily apparent

Only known to the initiated.

Inaudible
as to remain so.

In sorrow or misfortune
there is consolation or relief.

A cheer
to solace sorrow.

Separation
10-10-2002

Let us prepare! sort for a purpose,
put apart. arrange into sections
set into units
discriminate our differences
disunite and divide, our special service
distinguish from a special ingredient
from a combination or mixture
withdraw and secede
cease to be obedient.

Dismiss:
from the party
in different directions
we start, over again
disengaged; therefore, we coexist.

Individual form and function
severed thought, in junction
as an entity
solitary articles
coordinated in various combinations
shared and held in common distinctions
we set apart our connection.

I come apart
at the seams
what does it mean? To be divided
from the start.

In between our being
we have brought about
specifically what we are seeing.

The hedge separates the yards
is it because,
It is hard
to retard
our convictions, of disregard
for each other.

Can we see the forest
from the trees
the dust and the dampness
below and above the freeze?

Is foliage forgetful
a fetish or fornication
for a man and woman
an admiration
of regretfullness
a mirage a menagerie of glass
to pass, with emptiness of
foil, foil and flask?

Serenity
05-19-2005

The phenomenon
of finding valuable things
inevitably can mean
the glory of being
serene.

Thy will be done.

The quality of the state
of utter calm
the moon in full glory
a condition of expanse
can you relate?

Think of the time and the date.
Only take a glance
The water flows from the volcano
very warm.

Ruffled to the response
untroubled and clear of the clouds
having a smooth, clear face
you are pronounced.
Bound to the soil, and very proud
relevant to everything
that has taken place.

The serene condition of the expanse
will ever last.
A continuous flow
of the upside-down hourglass
free of storms
and unpleasant change
the turmoil remains the same.
You can be forewarned.

The part of a title
torn between two pages
in a place, where the breeze
bends the leaves
and branches with different shades of green
sway,
and there are apples
everywhere, soft, sour, and brittle.

Significant
09-29-2001

How meaningful are you to me
or am I to you?
Can you express your true
feelings and emotions to me?
If so, then momentous
will be my significance of
sharing and conveying my caring for you.

It is suggestive, consequence
a compassionate and hidden observance
a departure from chance
something that is different
attributed to special circumstance.

How hidden are our motives?
Are we archaic with our variance
our characteristic, contention
of our measurement of time?
Is it too large to chance, too reasonable
What is the weight of our importance?

Solitude
07-08-2000

Together we are
in a state
of being isolated.
Our condition stresses loneliness
We are distant, from each other
remotely alone.

Our physical separation
stresses circumstances
beyond seclusion, detachment
alienation, immeasurable
confiding intercourse
within a world of darkness.

The mirrors reflect shadows
shades of light and dark
white and gray and spare jet black
and all the intergrades of visions.

In between
those thin lines of separation
are void.

The force of our contact
completely distorts any other
combination of equations.

Oneself to oneself
we are no one.
Entity to entity
we are eternal
outside ourselves
we are inside each other.

The
04-29-2006

It is a definite article
quite a spectacle.
something well known
unique and oblique.
As the word is shown
as in the thought of the.
For you and me to see.

Generically, it is a class of individuals,
specifically.

Indicate one particular decade,
and include the charade,
dress in the costume,
and presume
we are all passing in the parade.

From the sublime, to the ridiculous,
where are thee, going in your time?

Are you superstitious?
Or is it none of the above?

what shall I presume?
Is it the thought of your resolve?

Note; a personal belonging.
Are you wanting,

for the part of the body and
the ultimate sensation?
Are you ready, for the ultimate inspiration?

I see the light, far out of sight,
it must be very bright!

Consistent with the night,
there is only a dimmer,
a trickle.

The Deep, Deep Sea
09-01-2009

How sweet it was
between you and me.

Underneath the crest
of the creamy, cool sea,
we were tangled up together.

We twirled and we twisted.
Turning the tide
of the deep blue-green sea.

The break of the wave
bellowed upon us.

Fancy, fresh, and floating free.

There we were
you and me.

Out in the undertow
of the splashing
splendorous sea.

Our thoughts were simple
and single minded,
they were of each other.
Completely, carefree
from here to eternity
a ripple in wave
flooding, tangled up
between us.

The Paradox of Prism
11-03-1996

Then seemed to be a contradiction
about the possible truth.
The expression
was an absurd statement.
Facial features were transparent
blushing red, glowing yellow, red-hot blue.

The proposition
was a solid base
with a parallel end
There were different angles
of the parallelograms and polygons.

The nature of the situation
exhibiting an apparent inconsistency
The faces were beginning to form
crystal clear.

The horizontal and vertical axes
intersecting, dividing.

The moon is in opposition to the sun
with Earth directly between them.

The question was a proposal.

Time
12-28-04

Your time is my time.
What time is it?
Time is running out.
How many times have I told you what to do?
It is every moment there has been or ever will be.
I find that the older I get. the faster time goes by.
Are you having the time of your life?
Why do they call a wristwatch a time piece?
It is all a matter of time.
Time is of the essence.
According to the theory of relativity, time is constant.
People say that time goes by too fast or too slow.
Time flies when you're having fun.
You're late for work again.
You are going to get fired.
Tardiness is timeless.
You must arrive in a timely fashion.
Meet the late John Doe.
Time is the enemy of youth and the friend of the elderly.
With reference to a characteristic social structure, with a set of
customs.

There are:
Prehistoric times
Medieval times
Geological times
Lincoln's time
A period characterized by a prevailing condition or specific ex-
perience.
A time for peace.
A time for war.
Good times and bad times.
From here to eternity.
There is always another time.
Take the time out.
Can we spend some quiet time together?

Time is money.
Stop wasting my time.
Times Square 42nd Street.
Let's make the most of our time here.
Time is the crucible of life experience.
There is time off for good behavior, after doing hard time.
On that note, I will have another beer.
Between the times now and then occasionally.
They are not punching the clock.
I am having one hell of a time here now.
Before it is too late, let's set the rhythm, the tempo, the pace.
One's own time.
How can I pass the time of day?
Time and again I have told you what is going to happen to you.
I have nothing to do.
Where have you gone to?
A period in the history of mankind and the universe.
Do you remember a famous person, or a friend, a person close
too, living then, there, or now.
I have a prevailing experience, with my existence.
I must be persistent, with the use of my time.
This is the end of our time together.

Transcend
12-07-2004

Beyond the limits of overstep
to surpass, excel
transcends belief of what we perceive
to be the ultimate preparation.

Apart from the material
the possible experience
the existence
beyond supernatural.

The necessary conditions were they
are they superstition?

Human knowledge
with rational algebraic equations
functional, exponential
with calibrations and permutations
and variations from what we have learned
our allegiance we must pledge:

Categories of the mind
declares freedom
and immortality in kind
sometimes, implied.

Jumping and running, dancing
around the carousel
we could not tell
what was forthcoming.

How green it may seem
to the lion.
Never, never to be in the land,
away from the birds, the living things.
Where in the forest with the leaves
on the trees, where the elephants

gleam and the sunlight is flowing with
a bright beam.

Can you smell the roses?
Red, white, purple, and pink,
orange and yellow and white
and blue, can you think?

Suppose the colors
were for us and the others?

Unfathomable
07-02-2000

How deep bluish green
my emotions are for you
I sway from tide to tide
eddie to eddie, crest to crest.

My league is unfathomable
for your depth.
I am calm and still and motionless
in the rain, in the night.

The water becomes brightfully full
of eyes looking and blinking and
persistently flinching.

My eyes are flux,
because they are full of flirtation
from you.
You are streamlined
straight and narrow
directly ahead of me, we collide.

I am crushed by your gleaming,
gorgeous glide into my sight.

We are sound and clear
cool and calm
We combine our fluids
and liquids and entities, together.

Venus
01-11-2007

You, you, you!
Are you of love and beauty?
Exceptionally true?

In the order of breasts,
the figure of the belly,
carving the buttocks,
how was I to know
so soft and smooth!
I always think of how
to caress and taste
the sweetness of jelly,
I am blessed.

Hence! the exciting qualities
of desire.
In the caverns
of medieval legend
I suppose of being
inhabited by Venus.

Delicate is the maidenhair,
I trust I am not in despair,
to submit to the orbit of Venus.
So beautiful and so fair.

There is no period of evolution
when the moon is in revolution,
that shades the second order
from the sun as Venus.

Brilliant with brightness and
exciting with charm.
Full of forgetfulness.
Tempting togetherness.
Delightfully warm.

A figure statuette,
smooth as ivory.
Picturesque, and so tasty.

Personifying!
Sexual!
Attractiveness!
Enticing!

Victual
03-20-2003

There are other provisions.
I live to feed
with a supply
of need
and decisions.

Articles are special
prepared for use.
Quick and fast
supplied to last,
with profusions.

Mix and mead,
use all of the ingredients
pursuant to the greed
of the recipients.

Innkeeper
can you lend me an ear
for I am in a clear
predicament,
of the resentment of my beard,
in the beer with the scent.

The pine in the park
and the wine and the whiskey
the turkey and the sark
the bush and the dork
of the maker's mark
who drinks
may or may not
be berserk!

Village
02-12-2004

In a country house
smaller than a city
the people are petite
developed for looking pretty,
each couple are sincere
and pleased with their spouse.

The habitation of animals and birds
are heard and seen, in between
the flowers and the trees
the cry of the owl
is heard.

Ownership of each other
is better, than to be bothered
smothered and covered
forever in a cluster
together.

Organized farming
we plow and mead the seed
everything grows green
it is simply charming.

Communication is collective
in the community
incorporated
protective
for the honest citizens
the contribution
is imperative.

Wealth
01-17-2004

I have a lot of money
a great amount of worldly possessions
an abundance of obsessions.

Derivative of the oceans
the unfathomable debts
prosperous and suggestive
I feel as if I am floating
and most wet and inept
out of sorts, full of promotions.

Some winners are extreme
to what it may seem
as an abundance
in nuance.

Sold or stocked
capable of being bought
what sort
of provocative
experience
are we to procrastinate
for the risk
of being caught
and blocked in lock?

What are my worldly possessions?
My material things?
Having something or nothing?
Is it my obsession?
As simple as it may seem?

Word
11-27-2008

Express your accent
tell your emotions in your words
bits and bytes
are always a present delight.
Meaning the absurd
you can always voice your intent.

In so many words
unequivocal terms
trustworthy and reliable.

Upon your surprise
some said a profane curse,
to be literal and true
as free and full of form perturbed.

A spoken sound
expression or utterance
authoritative in command,
can you understand
the meaning of profound?

Are you angry,
contentious in speech?

If you are true, blue to your word,
then justice
is as tall as a mountain,
as that of a thin man
can sing to a tune.

Ice skating in a figure of eight,
I hear the words *ding dong!*
As if there is a bell hanging
from a tree in the woods.
Where there is a monkey

swinging back and forth from a branch.
Aren't these blades on the boots great!

The chocolate factory
is fun for everyone.
Charlie knows how creamy and crunchy it is.
You can take the words right out of your mouth,
a good and plenty of them
express them exactly.

Xylophone
06-04-2004

The instrument
The notes
I quote:
"Implement with the bars bent"

Strike the keys
the music
I believe, plays
as you please.

The series
in length, is spent
upon the strike
of the hammer

as you may need
to apply in speed
when the hit
is where you believe
it to be with a dent.

Can you hear the sound
of the tune?

How soon will the bars graduate
and not be profound?

Bang the beginning
of the sound and the song
continuously bringing
what is right and wrong
to the listener all along.

You
04-03-2007

You are the light!
A beam so bright
a fire that burns
in the night.

Try to discover
the hidden you,
so that the sky
may be a clear blue bright.

We used to be in a place
up close and very personal
in our very special space.

As near as you are to me
somewhere, sometime
there was the distance
between the forest and the trees.

You have always been the one,
one of us.
Whom shall tell everything
about our family?
For we will be eternally,
as close as we can come together undone.

To two or more people
or to one person
you are incredible.

I will see you again
and then you will know,
because I will show you
how much I care
and since when.

You must make clear
the distinction between me and you.
Whom are you true to?

Somewhere, sometime, someplace,
where are you now, my dear?
So close and so far from our grace.

Youth

12-29-2003

Vigorous, vitality
lively, surely
being young
at an early stage
of maturity
is laughter and fun
for just about everyone.

The period of life
that is impetuous
and not so serious
suitable for fruitful
flirtation without strife.

Are we active and true
akin to a new
experience for me and you, too?

See the face
of the beginning
in such a place
that the future is for us
to embrace.

Fresh full of
our flavor of taste
between childhood and
the race, of human
existence of space
we are free to be
whom we see indefinitely.

Zenith
05-17-2004

The point in the sky
way up high
look and see
beyond pleasantly
far and fine
I wonder why.

Reaching the peak
of the sphere
very near
can I hear?
To be blue-green
and not seek
what I fear everywhere.

If I am in error
will I remember
as always
forever
to change things
for the better?

The road, the path
the way for today
where is the day
that it may last.

Directly opposite
the nadir
I bear, experience
the insight, the light
the brightness
in predicate.